Ethan Foster

The Conscript Quakers

Ethan Foster

The Conscript Quakers

ISBN/EAN: 9783337404710

Printed in Europe, USA, Canada, Australia, Japan

Cover: Foto ©Lupo / pixelio.de

More available books at **www.hansebooks.com**

THE

CONSCRIPT QUAKERS,

BEING A

NARRATIVE OF THE DISTRESS AND RELIEF
OF FOUR YOUNG MEN FROM THE
DRAFT FOR THE WAR IN 1863.

BY

ETHAN FOSTER.

CAMBRIDGE:

Printed at the Riverside Press.

1883.

At a meeting for Sufferings of New England Yearly Meeting of Friends, held at Pawtucket, R. I., 8th month 1st, 1883, Ethan Foster presented to this meeting a narrative in manuscript of the efforts made by himself and Charles Perry in 1863 for the relief of four young men who were drafted to go into the army ; which their conscientious scruples forbade them to do. The friends named were members of a Committee of South Kingstown Monthly Meeting, in R. I., appointed to have the care of such cases. The narrative has been read to our satisfaction, and Ethan Foster is left at liberty to publish it, with the approval of this meeting.

JEREMIAH FOSTER, CLERK.

NOTE. It is expected that this little narrative may fall into the hands of many who are not familiar with Friends and their methods. For such this note is made.

The Society of Friends very early established a representative body, in each Yearly Meeting, called *"The Meeting for Sufferings,"* to have a special care in cases of the hard treatment and suffering of any, on account of their maintaining our principles; and to afford relief if possible. This meeting is continued under the same name, and has general care for the welfare of the Society; of latter times, perhaps, more especially, in regard to what may be published touching its doctrines and testimonies. This name may seem unsuitable for a meeting; but we apprehend that whoever may read a little book recently published, entitled "The Quaker Invasion of Massachusetts," by Richard P. Hallowell, setting forth the treatment of Friends by the Puritans, in an able and unanswerable manner, will be convinced of the need of such a body, and that its name was appropriate and well chosen.

ETHAN FOSTER,
CHARLES PERRY.

WESTERLY, R. I., *8th mo. 1st,* 1883.

THE CONSCRIPT QUAKERS.

In the summer of 1863, the Government of the United States ordered a draft, for the purpose of increasing the force to put down the rebellion in the Slave States. The laws of Rhode Island, as also those of some of the other states which had exempted Friends from military service, were, under the extraordinary excitement attending the draft, suddenly repealed.[1] But even had this not been done, the government order, issued as it was in time of war, would probably have overruled the state laws. The fact that they were repealed shows

[1] See note at the end.

the strong feeling of intolerance which, in the agitation of the time, prevailed in regard to the conscientious scruples of Friends against being concerned in war.

It is not my purpose to consider the reasons why so few were, in consequence of this condition of affairs, brought into trouble, like those of whom I am now more particularly to speak. There is abundant evidence that the well known testimony of the Society of Friends against war was sadly disregarded, not only in New England, but throughout the whole country. This seems generally to have been done by the payment, either directly or indirectly, on the part of the drafted persons, of the commutation (three hundred dollars), which by law exempted them from serving : this amount being used to hire a substitute.

The delinquency in sustaining this particular testimony of the Society was doubtless owing in great measure to the general and almost universal departure, of late years, from many other of our primitive and vital testimonies.

It was under these circumstances that several members of the smaller body in New England were drafted.[2] Some of these were exempted on account of physical disability. Two members of Rhode Island Quarterly Meeting, however, were held; as were two others — one a young man from Maine, then at the Providence Boarding School, and the other a " Rogerine," so called, a sect which also renounces war; and is principally located

[2] This smaller body, or Yearly Meeting, was the result of a separation in 1845 on doctrinal issues ; the smaller body being sometimes termed Wilburites from John Wilbur, who took a prominent part in opposing innovation in doctrine into the Society.

at Groton, Connecticut. The cases of
these young men were taken in charge
by a committee of South Kingstown (R.
I.) Monthly Meeting of Friends, appointed for the purpose, and Charles
Perry and myself were designated to act
on their behalf and obtain relief if possible.

We had several interviews with the
state authorities — the Governor (James
Y. Smith), and the Provost Marshal
(Alfred B. Chadsey), both of whom manifested much sympathy for our suffering
friends, and expressed a willingness to
do whatever they could to help them.
They finally recommended that we
should lay the case before the President
of the United States. In accordance
with this advice we went to Washington
not long after the battle of Gettysburg.
President Lincoln received us kindly,

but said he did not see how he could
grant our friends exemption from military service, without so far "*letting
down the bars*" as to render nugatory
all his efforts to crush the rebellion.
Upon being told that we did not look
upon it in that light, he said it amounted
to that; dwelt much on the difficulties
which would attend the exemption of
any portion of those by law subject to
draft; said that if he began, there would
be no stopping place; spoke of the difficulties with which he was beset on every
hand; of the trouble he was having with
the Governor of New York on account
of the draft in that state; said he had
not time to give attention and thought
to these matters; that before one thing
was duly considered and digested, another
of a totally different character was presented and pressed upon his attention;

that anything he might do or say to-day would be in the public papers to-morrow, and be heralded from Maine to Georgia. At length, however, he said that he " should be very unwilling for any truly conscientious person to be made to suffer ; " immediately adding, " *but even this must not be repeated.*" He finally asked, " What *can* we do for you ? I don't see what we *can* do." I replied that our Governor suggested that he might think it would do to release these men on parole ; to hold them subject to call. At this he was silent for some time and made no reply to the remark ; but I thought it struck him favorably, and that if anything was ultimately done, this course might be pursued.

The President said it would not do to make a special exception in the case of Friends ; that there were others who professed to be conscientiously opposed to war. We acknowledged this, and expressed a hope that if any favors were granted, it would be done impartially. I remarked, however, that I nevertheless thought the claims of the Society of Friends stronger than those of any other class, from the fact that they had long since abolished slavery within their own borders; and that if every other of the religious denominations had done the same, we should not have had this war; to which he replied, "*You never said a truer thing than that.*" [3]

Immediately after what was said about releasing the men on parole, the President said to his clerk, " Take down the

[3] The Society of Friends in America made the holding of slaves a disownable offence, about the year 1780 ; the Yearly Meeting of Philadelphia as early as 1776. See Greeley's *American Conflict*, vol. i., p. 117, 118.

names of the men on whose behalf these gentlemen are here, and put the paper where you can lay your hand on it." When, in the course of the conversation, I remarked that I did not know that any Friends had been forced into the rebel army by Jeff. Davis, he replied, "Yes there have, for we liberated five a few days since, who were taken prisoners at the battle of Gettysburg, and were then confined in Fort Delaware."

He advised us to consult the Secretary of War in regard to the matter, and gave us a note of introduction to Secretary Stanton. He said he did not know whether any order had been given that would affect cases of this kind. Upon taking leave of the President we asked if we could see him again, after our interview with the Secretary of War, should we desire it. "Oh, yes," he said, "come right here and I will see you again."

Secretary Stanton received us courteously, and we opened to him the object of our call ; stated what the President had said as to whether or not any order had been issued to meet such cases. He replied, " *No, and there can be none.*" We set forth as well as we could the distress of our young friends, in being called on for service in the war, which they could not in conscience perform. The Secretary gave little or no encouragement that he could help us out of our troubles, but he told us that his own parents were *Friends*, and spoke of those they had liberated from Fort Delaware, of whom the President had told us ; said that Thomas Evans (a Friend of Philadelphia whom we knew) came to Washington on their behalf, etc. The Provost Marshal (Fry) also treated us with much civility.

Soon after we entered the War Office, the Secretary of State (Wm. H. Seward) came in and took a seat. He remained silent until our conference with Secretary Stanton was concluded; when Charles Perry (who had an impression that Seward, when Governor of New York, had recommended the passage of a law to exempt from military service those who were conscientiously opposed to war) turned to him expecting a word of sympathy and encouragement, and remarked that he would perceive why we were there; upon which he suddenly and with much vehemence of manner asked, "Why don't the Quakers fight?" Charles replied, "Because they believe it wrong, and cannot do it with a clear conscience." He reprimanded us severely because we refused to fight. After a little pause I said, "Well, if this world were all, per-

haps we might take thy advice;" to
which he responded, " The way to get
along well in the next world is to do
your duty in this." I replied, " That is
what we are trying to do; and now, I
want to ask thee one question, and I
want thee to answer it; whose preroga-
tive is it to decide what my duty is,
thine or mine?" He did not answer the
question, but became more angry and
excited; asked, " Why, then, don't you
pay the commutation?" We told him
we could see no difference between the
responsibility of doing an act ourselves
and that of hiring another to do it for
us. On this he sprang from his seat and
strided around in a circle of some eight
or ten feet across, exclaiming, *"Then I'll
pay it for you,"* and thrusting his hand
into his coat pocket, added, *" I'll give
you my check!"*

Immediately after this exhibition, we took our leave in much sadness, at treatment so opposite to that we had expected from Secretary Seward.

We went directly to the President's house and found him ready to receive us pleasantly and kindly. We told him what Secretary Stanton had said as to the impossibility of an order being given to meet such cases as these; which was, indeed, no more than we had anticipated. We told the President that we had met with Secretary Seward at the War Office and of his harsh treatment of us; that we were very glad of this second opportunity to see *him*, for we feared that the strong feelings of Secretary Seward against us might have an unfavorable influence with him. He was walking the room at the time, and on hearing this, raised his head suddenly, and said with a smile, " Oh! he wouldn't say half as much to me when you were gone." After some further talk in which his sympathy with us was plainly manifested, I think I may say we took an affectionate leave of him.

On our return we stopped at Philadelphia, to learn what further we could of the five Friends who had been in the rebel army. We went to the house of Thomas Evans, where they were staying, kindly cared for by himself and others. We had much conversation with them of great interest; found that they had persistently refused to bear arms, or to do anything that would implicate them in taking the lives of their fellow-men. Four of them had been treated with a good degree of consideration; no effort having been made to compel them to bear arms. But one had fallen into the

2

hands of a hardened and cruel officer, who treated him with severity, to the extent even of riding his horse against him, thus throwing him down and riding over him, without, however, doing him any material injury. The horse was more merciful than his rider, and refused to step on him. When he rose, the officer said to him with an oath, " I have not done with you yet. I will either make you fight or I will kill you." At one time he drew up a corps of his men in file, and ordered them to shoot him. In this extremity the young man exclaimed, " Father, forgive them; they know not what they do." The soldiers were reached, and refused to obey, saying, " We cannot shoot this man." This was but a short time before the battle of Gettysburg, early in which engagement, this officer was killed; and the non-com-

batants were sent to the rear. The
rebels were obliged to retreat, and these
Friends being found after the battle
were taken prisoners as already stated.

We stayed over First-day at Thomas
Evans' and attended their ~~Monthly~~ *Quarterly* Meeting in Philadelphia on Second-day; then
returned home.

The conscripted young men were soon
summoned to camp, whither Provost
Marshal Chadsey advised that they be
allowed to go, as a choice of evils, between that, and their being taken as
prisoners to Governor's Island (a military station in New York harbor), to be
disposed of as might there be determined. He said they were old *military
stagers* at Governor's Island, who knew
little aside from military operations and
tactics, and would have little or no idea
of lenity or mercy. But we thought if

they went into camp they might be summarily ordered away, beyond our reach; and further, that we might as well know the worst at once; that if they were to be tried by court-martial as deserters, it might as well come first as last. We therefore decided to go with them to Governor's Island; and did so, under feelings of intense anxiety and much doubt as to the result.

Before seeing the Commandant, who was a Colonel Loomis, we happened to meet with the physician and the surgeon, both of whom, after hearing our story, at once took part with us. We found that the former was well acquainted with Friends, his wife being a member of the Society; and that the latter was a man of more than ordinary ability, and of very kindly feelings. On coming before the Colonel, the surgeon at once volunteered to plead our cause, saying, "Colonel, it will never do to send such men as these over to the castle;[4] they are of the respectable and intelligent class of society ; " to which the Colonel replied, " *That* is what I should like to avoid." After hearing our plea, he said he should send us over to General Canby, who had charge of the troops in the city. The surgeon (Dr. White) asked the Colonel if he might go with us to General Canby's headquarters, saying that we should need a guide. To this a ready assent was given, I need not say greatly to our satisfaction.

General Canby listened considerately to our plea, but said he thought we might pay the commutation without any

---

[4] A place which we subsequently visited, and found it filled with an apparently vile and hardened set; among them many from the lowest classes in the city.

sacrifice of principle; that it was put into the law purposely to meet such cases. We replied that we could see no difference between taking up arms ourselves and hiring others to do it in our places; that by the law this commutation was to be used to hire a substitute. He did not seem disposed to discuss the question, and soon said: " Well, I can pretty easily appreciate your scruples; my near relations are mostly Friends; " when Charles Perry said, " It is very singular that we meet so many who are connected with Friends in our calls upon military men; that the Secretary of War told us that his *parents* were Friends." General Canby soon said he thought it best to write the President and lay the case before him. He then wrote to Colonel Loomis on the Island, and handed the letter folded but unsealed to Charles

Perry, who was about to put it in his pocket, when General Canby said to him, " *Read it;* " which Charles then did; and with much feeling said, " It is all we could ask; if I had written it myself I could not have put it in more satisfactory terms." The letter was to this effect: That he had decided to refer the case of these men to the President, for his judgment; and meanwhile, until he received an answer, the Colonel was directed to retain them on the Island, with no other restriction than their *word* that they would not leave; and that nothing should be required of them inconsistent with their principles.

We left General Canby with a comfortable hope that we should get a favorable decision; knowing that when President Lincoln saw the names of the men, he would find, by reference to the list his clerk had taken, that they were the same ; and that he would remember our interviews with him. We then went back to the Island, and leaving the young men there, returned home. After waiting more than two weeks, and hearing nothing from General Canby, who was to advise us of any tidings he might receive, we again went to New York to learn what further we could. We first called on the General, who said he had been expecting letters for some time, but had as yet received none. We then went to the Island and saw the young men, who were a good deal discouraged, fearing they would have to remain there during the war. We left them and went to Flushing, Long Island, to stop with our relatives there, promising to return next morning and spend the First-day with them. On going back next morning, wnen nearing the Island, we saw the young men standing on the wharf, looking very cheerful. On landing they informed us that an order had been received from Washington for their release! They had a copy of the order, and passed it to us to read. It required that these men be discharged on parole until they should be called for. Surgeon White was with them on the wharf, and appeared no less joyful than the rest; he asked whether we knew what "*until they are called for*" meant; adding, "it means that they will *never* be called for." We told him that we so understood it. Taking leave of him with due acknowledgment of his kindness in this time of trial, we immediately left the Island. Our young friends went with us to Flushing, where we stayed until the next day. Upon our return to the city,

we again called on General Canby, and
thanked him for the kindness which he
had shown us, and the interest he had
manifested on our behalf; far beyond
what we had reason to expect.

We took the evening boat for home;
and I never remember to have spent a
more joyful day and night in my life.
My peace flowed as a river, and a song
of thanksgiving unutterable was raised
unto Him whose Almighty Hand was
clearly discernible throughout these re-
markable occurrences.

Provost Marshal Chadsey, on being
informed of the kind and feeling recep-
tion, which we met at Governor's Island
and in New York city, and of the final
result, exclaimed, "You were right and
I was wrong;" and added, "It really
seems as if the Divine Hand was in it."

The young men went to their several

homes, and continued to pursue their ordinary avocations until the end of the
war. No call was ever made for them
by the government.

No doubt the faithfulness we were en-
abled to pursue in going to Governor's
Island was a great aid in the removal of
our difficulties. We have, in the experi-
ence we met with from the authorities of
the land, and especially from the military officers, a striking illustration of the
great advance in religious toleration and
freedom which has been made since the
early settlement of our country; and a
forcible reminder that we of this gener-
ation owe much to the unflinching in-
tegrity and faithfulness of our early
Friends; even unto death, in support of
our testimonies.

Note. We are glad to acknowledge that the Charter of
Rhode Island, granted to Roger Williams and his asso-

ciates for the organization of the government of that colony in 1663, provided for "*full liberty in religious concernments*" (a very comprehensive term); and that however much the laws in times of excitement may have swerved from this only true ground, yet it has ever been the prevailing policy of its people from that day to this. These original settlers, as well as those of Pennsylvania, under the auspices of William Penn and the early Friends, exhibited to the natives the Christian virtues they professed; bought and paid for the soil they occupied, and otherwise treated them with fairness and honesty. They thus secured the good-will and kind offices of the native tribes; and it was not until differences arose between the Indians of Rhode Island, under the rule of the celebrated King Philip, and the European settlers of Plymouth and Massachusetts, who were sympathized with and aided by those of Connecticut, that hostilities commenced; culminating in the great swamp fight near the close of the year 1675, in which the Indians were most cruelly destroyed, both by the carnage of war and by fire. The "New American Cyclopedia," vol. xiv., page 53, says, "Rhode Island was opposed to this exterminating war, and was not even consulted in regard to it by the other colonies."

The following extract from the Charter of Rhode Island shows upon what broad and tolerant ground its government was founded. The King (Charles II.) in the opening clause of the charter, speaking of the settlers, says: "And whereas in their humble address they have freely declared, that it is much on their hearts (if they may be permitted) to hold forth a lively experiment that a most flourishing civil state may stand and best be maintained, and that among our English subjects, with a full liberty in religious concernments; and that true piety, rightly grounded upon gospel principles, will give the best and greatest security to sovereignty, and will lay in the hearts of men the strongest obligations to true loyalty: Now know ye," etc.; goes on, "to secure them in the free exercise and enjoyment of all their civil and religious rights," etc.

The Government of Rhode Island was continued under this original charter until the year 1842, when it was followed by the present Constitution, which fully recognizes the same sound and noble principles as the foundation of the state.